TROUBLE WiTH SCHOOL

A Family Story About Learning Disabilities

Kathryn Boesel Dunn & Allison Boesel Dunn

Illustrations by Rick Stromoski

WOODBINE HOUSE 1993

Library of Congress Cataloging-in-Publication Data

Dunn, Kathryn Boesel.
  Trouble with school : a family story about learning disabilities /
by Kathryn Boesel Dunn & Allison Boesel Dunn ; illustrated by
Rick Stromoski.
     p.   cm.
  ISBN 0–933149–57–3 (paper) : $9.95
  1. Learning disabled children—United States—Case studies. 2.
Learning disabled children—Education (Primary)—United States—
Case studies. 3. Dunn, Kathryn Boesel. 4. Dunn, Allison Boesel. I.
Dunn, Allison Boesel. II. Stromoski, Rick. III. Title.
LC4705.D86 1993   92–40394
371.97—dc20   CIP

Manufactured in Hong Kong

10 9 8 7 6 5 4 3 2 1

Introduction

This is the story of my family's discovery of learning disabilities in the primary grades. Although learning disabilities are common, for each child and family they are a personal, troublesome experience. After my daughter was diagnosed as learning disabled, I talked with experts and searched for materials. I especially looked for books at the primary level that would help my daughter understand this disability, but found they were scarce.

As we went through the process of adjusting to our daughter's diagnosis and its implications, we were angry, sad, confused, and finally relieved to define the problem and work toward a solution. Experts we've worked with tell us these are common family reactions. This book is about our experience. By sharing our story, we hope to help other families in much the same way we gained support and information from talking with other parents of learning disabled children. We hope this book will provide insight and understanding to others faced with similar circumstances.

Allison tells the story in her own words. My annotations provide a different perspective. The back of the book contains a resource guide with information about associations that we found helpful.

—*Kathryn Boesel Dunn*

Allison's Mother's Story

By every indication, Allison should have been a wildly successful student. She talked early, in complete sentences before she was two years old. Friends and family were amazed at her vocabulary and zest for life.

As a toddler she was hard to keep up with, but she listened avidly to stories every night. She started preschool at three and made friends easily—with both older and younger children. She was outgoing and popular.

She loved kindergarten and looked forward to first grade, where she hoped to learn to read like her older sister. But when she got to first grade, she didn't love it. She didn't like the fact that there was no housekeeping corner and she didn't pick up reading as I expected, but I hoped that maturity would solve the problem. She finished first grade behind the other students.

In second grade, the problems intensified.

Allison's Story

I was having a terrible time with school. Nothing seemed to go right. Almost every morning before school there was a **terrible** scene at home.

I didn't want to get up. I didn't want to get dressed. I didn't want to eat breakfast. I didn't want to go to school.

Allison's Mother's Story

I remember those first few weeks of second grade. They were awful. I knew Allison would have a hard time adjusting to the school schedule. She wasn't a morning person and she loved the freedom and play of summer.

The first few weeks of second grade were even worse than expected. No matter how early I started, I couldn't get her out of bed. She cried, she balked at dressing, she refused to eat breakfast, she argued with everyone who crossed her path. My husband and I did our share of arguing with her too.

By the time Allison and I arrived at school we were both exhausted and upset. Driving home I sometimes cried, wondering what was wrong with Allison.

Allison's Story

My mom, my dad, my sister, and I were all fighting. The noise, the fussing, and the arguing that went on before school was just awful!

"Allison, I don't know why you have such a horrible time getting up in the morning. I'm going to have to put you to bed earlier so you aren't so slow and grumpy in the morning," my mom said.

"Allison, I don't know why you are making such a fuss this morning. It's ruining everyone's day," my dad said.

"Allison, stay out of my room and my closet. You aren't allowed to take my clothes. I don't want you in my room!" my sister said.

Nobody understood I didn't want to go to school. But my mom and dad said I had to go, so I went. I was usually tardy.

Allison's Mother's Story

Although I was studying for a master's degree in reading, I didn't know that Allison's emotional outbursts at home were caused by problems at school. I knew she was behind in reading, but I thought it might be a matter of emotional immaturity.

I discussed the problem with my college advisor and she reassured me that children develop at different rates. She said that reading to Allison was the best help I could give her. And so we read, lots of books, every night.

One of my college projects involved asking a child to first read a fable and then retell it in her own words. I used Allison and another child in the neighborhood. Allison remembers it as a reading failure. I had no idea she was embarrassed and worried about the project.

Allison's Story

In first grade I couldn't read the books that everyone else could. It seemed like the sentences would move and I would lose my place. So I would just look at the words and pretend I was reading. Kids made fun of me 'cause I couldn't read. Nobody liked me, and people talked about me like I was stupid. I only had one friend.

One time, when my mom was back in college, my friend and I helped her with her class project. We both read a story and then told it in our own words. I was really embarrassed because my friend could read it and I couldn't. I was mad at myself because I couldn't read, and he was younger than I was.

Allison's Mother's Story

Allison's second grade teacher was aware of her learning problems in those first few weeks. She referred Allison to a reading tutor program and recommended that we do some special testing.

Allison's father thought the teacher was wrong. His first reaction was, "That teacher doesn't know anything. Anyone can tell by talking to Allison how smart she is!" I knew that he was not going to believe that Allison had any sort of problem, especially one with learning.

I was defensive telling him about the teacher's recommendations. I told him that research shows that teacher observations are often the most reliable assessment of problems. They are almost always as valid as tests. Andy gave in gracefully and agreed that we needed to find out more about what was happening to Allison.

Allison's Story

In second grade, everybody was saying, "Allison, why aren't you paying attention? Allison, why don't you listen to me? Allison, how many times do I have to tell you? Allison, you aren't trying!"

I didn't understand why my mom would make me suffer and go to school. I was angry at her. Why couldn't we change schools? I didn't like myself. I thought I was stupid.

My teacher knew I was having trouble, so she sent me to a special reading class. But I knew it wasn't the right place for me. The teacher asked my parents if they could give me some tests to find out more about the problem.

Allison's Mother's Story

We consulted several experts about Allison's problems—our pediatrician, two eye specialists, and a child psychologist. The school had its own team made up of the school psychologist, the learning disabilities teacher, the principal, and Allison's teacher.

Part of the school's testing included an emotional assessment. We preferred to have our independent child psychologist do that. The school put our private psychologist on the team. The school tested for learning disabilities, and then we waited. It was awful. The school psychologists had lots of kids to test. It was hard to wait, and meanwhile the problems didn't get any better.

Allison's Story

When I found out I was going to be tested, I was scared. I was afraid the tests would show I had a problem. I didn't want to be tested because I didn't want to be different. I just wanted to be like all the other kids.

But my parents wanted me to take the tests, so I did. The tests were weird. The school psychologist asked me to draw a triangle and I drew it. It looked different from the other triangles and I didn't know why. I felt scared.

For the gym tests I had to walk up and down the stairs. Then I had to hang on the bars. I did pretty well with that stuff and I was proud.

Mom took me to see a lot of other people too. I went to the doctor and two eye doctors. I went to see a child psychologist. A child psychologist is a doctor, but not the kind that gives you shots or medicine when you're sick. She's a doctor who helps you with a special problem, like if you don't feel good about yourself.

I told my mom that I was sick and tired of all this testing!

Allison's Mother's Story

The school officials called us in for a team meeting to review Allison's test results. They said the tests showed that Allison was, indeed, very bright, but that she was having trouble in reading and in written expression. The discrepancy between her test scores and school performance showed that she had a learning disability. They were pleased to have found the problem and were confident that they could help.

We weren't so pleased. We didn't want to hear that our daughter had a learning disability. They gave us some papers on our rights as parents of a handicapped child. I didn't think she was handicapped, and I had certainly never considered a learning disability a handicap! (How wrong I was! A learning disability is truly the hidden handicap.)

At this meeting, the learning disabilities teacher explained her program for Allison and reviewed the school's suggested Individualized Education Program (IEP) for Allison.

There was so much information at the meeting I couldn't even speak. It was too much to assimilate in one session and we were overwhelmed. On the other hand, we were relieved to have the problem defined and to know the school was developing a strategy to help Allison learn.

Allison's Story

When the testing was all done, Mom and Dad went to a meeting at school to find out what the tests said. There were a lot of people there—my teacher, my principal, the school psychologist, the learning disabilities teacher, and the child psychologist. All of these people were worried about me. They didn't want me to have so much trouble with school. They said the tests showed I had a learning disability.

Allison's Mother's Story

We went home and talked with Allison about the team meeting. I stressed to her that she was not stupid. In fact tests proved she was very bright. I told her what I had learned in my diagnosis class: that many times when a bright child has low performance, it is a learning disability. In her case, that was the diagnosis that was made.

The next day our child psychologist called and reviewed the testing. I cried and then apologized for crying. She said it was a normal reaction. She said, "When you feel frustrated and upset, multiply that a lot and you'll understand what Allison is feeling."

Allison's Story

I asked my mom and dad:

- What is a learning disability?
- How do you get a learning disability?
- Am I stupid?
- What does all this mean?

My mom said, "Learning disabilities just are. Nobody knows what causes them or why people have them. They happen to both girls and boys.

"A learning disability means that it's harder for you to learn in some areas even when you try your best."

My mom said, "You're going to start seeing the learning disabilities teacher. She is sooooo nice. I know you are going to like her."

Allison's Mother's Story

The learning disabilities teacher uses different teaching techniques for each child based on his or her specific needs. Allison had problems with written expression and she was definitely not a visual learner. She could barely write two sentences about any subject!

To help Allison put her thoughts in writing, the teacher asked her to write sentences about a story on strips of paper. Allison then arranged these strips in sequence. This way, writing a story didn't seem so overwhelming. Three times a year, the teacher published the children's stories and poems and sent them home in a book. Allison was always very proud of this book. She began to bring work home from school to share with me. She seemed a little more organized, and quite a bit happier. Sending her to school wasn't quite so painful for her or for me.

Allison's Story

The next day I went to see the learning disabilities teacher. I was a little nervous, but when I got there I found out I wasn't alone. The other kids were friendly and made me feel at home.

My teacher was nice and she understood that some things were hard for me. She gave me things to do that I could do and helped me with the things I couldn't do. And, if I didn't understand, she explained again in a different way. I began to think that I was going to learn to read, and that it wouldn't be too hard.

Allison's Mother's Story

By the time testing was complete and Christmas vacation had passed, half a year was lost. Although Allison was making progress, it was slow going. It was obvious she was at the bottom of her class and might have to repeat second grade.

We worried for six months about the decision. Should we push her and tutor her, or should we let her repeat? We knew that the other children would make fun of her if we held her back, and we worried about her fragile self-esteem. On the other hand, the teacher said Allison did not have all of the skills she needed for third grade.

Our pediatrician finally asked the right question: "Where will Allison have more successes?"

Looking at it from that viewpoint, the answer was obvious. She repeated second grade.

Allison's Story

At the end of second grade, my parents went to a special meeting. Everybody was there again, and they all decided I should repeat the second grade.

I was upset because it made me feel stupid. I was mad at my mom and dad because they said it was up to them to make the final decision. I thought they were against me. Why wouldn't they let me go on to the third grade?

My mom and dad said that repeating second grade would be in my best interests. They told me I could pick whatever teacher I wanted for the second grade again. I was happy, but I felt rushed because I didn't have much time to decide who I wanted. I decided to ask for my same second grade teacher again.

Allison's Mother's Story

Allison's team had warned us when we met in May that retaining her in second grade would be difficult. They tried to prepare us, but no one can really get you ready for the trauma of school retention.

Allison was humiliated those first few weeks. She cried every day for the first week. She was angry, and being the verbal child she is, she had no trouble telling us what she thought of us and our decision. It was very painful to see her so upset, and my husband and I both felt heartsick.

Allison's Story

At the beginning of the next year, everybody in my class except one person said that I flunked and I was dumb. Every day for one week I would come home from school and cry. I said, "I hate you, Mom! Why did you and Dad make me stay back?" Mom and Dad told me that things would get better.

Allison's Mother's Story

When the team warned us about the trauma, they also told us it would pass quickly. They were right. Within the first few weeks everybody forgot it and Allison got down to work, tackling the skills she'd need for third grade.

Because she had repeated second grade and was receiving special education, I expected her to be at the top of her class and quite successful. She wasn't. She was stronger in some areas than others, but it was a year of slow growing for Allison. School got a little better and a little easier every day. I was beginning to understand that there are no quick solutions or cures for a child with a learning disability. Gradually, my feelings were getting easier to handle, and my expectations were becoming more realistic.

Allison's Story

After a while it was okay. I made some new friends and I still saw some of my old friends.

School was easier because of my learning disabilities teacher. In the special education class I worked with puzzles and mazes. I read easy books and we got to publish our own books. We got stamps for coming and bringing our pencils. If we filled up our stamp folder we got awards. After so many awards, the class got to go out to lunch.

I felt better because I knew I wasn't the only one who was having trouble with school. My life started to turn around. Finally, I finished second grade and was ready for third grade.

Allison's Mother's Story

In third grade I was determined to get Allison off to a good start. At the beginning of the year, we arranged for after-school tutoring two afternoons a week. I wanted her to do her big projects with the tutor rather than at home.

Our pediatrician said, "Allison needs a safe place where she doesn't have to worry about school." We try to make home that place.

This doesn't mean she isn't responsible for homework. She is. But sometimes it's difficult to get her to do it. After school she's tired and frustrated from concentrating in class all day. I usually give her a snack and send her outside to play before we begin homework.

Allison's Story

In third grade I was really excited because I got the teacher I wanted. I was upset because my best friend wasn't in my class. Both of us cried about it.

Third grade is different because there are more book reports and projects. This means more writing and that's hard for me. There aren't as many field trips, and you have to learn multiplication and division tables. My third grade teacher helped me get organized at school.

Allison's Mother's Story

Even though things seem to be going well, we still have a long haul ahead of us. Already, I am looking into ordering fourth-grade books on tape. I'm also looking for consumable textbooks in math so Allison doesn't have to recopy problems. We'll be ordering her own textbooks so main points can be highlighted.

With help, Allison has finally experienced some success in school, but she couldn't have done it without special education and the help of many people and organizations.

I once read that parents play the key role in assuring the success of their child's education. I believe this to be true. We are our child's best advocate. I urge you to get involved, and to work closely with your child's school and pediatrician. Seek outside help and professional advice. We found working with an independent child psychologist to be extremely helpful.

Organizations can also provide information and support. See the last page for a list of national organizations that can help. Contact them for the address of the local chapter nearest you.

Allison's Story

I worry about grades. I think grades are real important. Sentences still move sometimes when I'm reading, and writing is still my hardest subject. I know what I want to say and I can tell you, but I can't write it down.

I don't think I'm stupid anymore, but I still don't really understand what learning disability means. Some days I have trouble with school and some days I don't want to go to school. But most days I feel much better. My grades are good. I have a lot of friends, and the best thing this year is that I was elected to Student Council.

What Is a Learning Disability?

A learning disability (LD) is a life-long disorder which affects the manner in which individuals with normal or above average intelligence select, retain, and express information. Incoming or outgoing information may become scrambled as it travels between the senses and the brain.

Learning disabilities should be considered as a possible cause if a child has trouble with one or more of the following:

- thinking clearly
- spelling accurately
- learning to compute
- remembering facts
- putting things in sequence

- writing legibly
- learning to read
- copying forms
- following directions

or, if he is often confused, clumsy, impulsive, hyperactive, or disoriented, becoming frustrated and rebellious, depressed, withdrawn, or aggressive.

The Learning Disabilities Association of America estimates that about 5 to 10 percent of people in the U.S. today have some kind of learning disability. Some other organizations place the estimate as high as 20 percent.

The student with learning disabilities may require a variety of services which can include: tutorial services, special academic advisement, basic skill remediation, assistance in organization and development of adequate study skills, and additional program accommodation, or modification. Some students with learning disabilities may not require extensive use of personnel, extra funds, or assistance from teachers, but may need appropriate program modifications and use of auxiliary aids. These include readers, scribes, note-takers, extended time policies for assigned papers, projects, or tests, and taped books or lectures.

Public schools are required by law to provide persons with learning disabilities with a free, appropriate education. Good school systems are working in compliance with the law. Good professionals are dedicated to careful diagnosis and quality remediation. Programs and services for persons with learning disabilities are mandated through high school age and beyond, and should be available.

—Learning Disabilities Association of America

National Organizations

The Learning Disabilities
  Association of America
4156 Library Road
Pittsburgh, PA 15234
412–341–1515

Orton Dyslexia Society
Chester Building, Suite 382
8600 LaSalle Road
Baltimore, MD 21286
410–296–0232

CH.A.D.D.
Children with Attention
  Deficit Disorders
N.W. 70th Avenue
Suite 308
Plantation, FL 33317
305–587–3700

Council for Learning
  Disabilities
P.O. Box 40303
Overland Park, KS 66204
913–492–8755

National Center for Learning Disabilities
99 Park Avenue, 6th Floor
New York, NY 10016
212–687–7211